NEWNESS

A GUIDE TO RENEWING THE MIND AND
PUTTING OFF THE OLD MAN
...FOR GOOD

Newness: A Guide to Renewing the Mind and Putting Off the Old Man... for Good
Copyright © 2018 John B. Lowe II

All rights reserved. No part of this book may be used or reproduced by any means, graphic, electronic, mechanical, including photocopying, recording, taping, or by any information storage retrieval system without the written permission of the author except in the case of brief quotations embodied in critical articles and reviews.

All Scripture taken from the New King James Version®. Copyright © 1982 by Thomas Nelson. Used by permission. All rights reserved.

Pulpit to Page Publishing Co. books may be ordered through booksellers or by contacting:
Pulpit to Page Publishing Co.
USA & Abroad || P U L P I T T O P A G E . C O M

ISBN-13: 978-1724458995
ISBN-10: 172445899X

NEWNESS

A GUIDE TO RENEWING THE MIND AND
PUTTING OFF THE OLD MAN
...FOR GOOD

• • • • • • •

PASTOR JOHN B. LOWE II

For more information on the ministry of Pastor John B. Lowe II, write to or visit:

New Life Christian Church & World Outreach
744 S. 325 E. | Warsaw, IN 46582

(574) 269-5851

i h a v e n e w l i f e . c o m

CONTENTS

Introduction

Chapter One: Old Skin ... **1**

Chapter Two: The Catch-Up ... **11**

Chapter Three: Our Role ... **15**

Chapter Four: Staying vs. Straying ... **21**

Chapter Five: Mandatory Maturity ... **29**

Chapter Six: Developing Your Soil ... **37**

Chapter Seven: The Cost ... **45**

Meet the Author ... **49**

INTRODUCTION

Occasionally when we hear a familiar sermon title or read a teaching, we are tempted to be quick to judge the subject matter as "old news." We say, "I've heard all this before. I know it already." However, the kingdom is about hearing it… not once, but *again* and *again* and *again* and *again*! Faith comes by hearing the Word… not *having heard* the Word.

The Apostle Paul said, "Finally, my brethren, rejoice in the Lord. For me to write the same things to you is not tedious, but for you it is safe" (Philippians 3:1). There is safety in repetition.

Putting off the old man might not sound like the most thrilling venture. It might sound like a dated topic that you've already become acquainted with. However, the principles of God are not dated, they're *eternal*. Putting off the old man can be painful and trying. However, it'll change your life. It's the core-key of sanctification. When we neglect this daily practice, we quickly start to look like the old man despite that fact that we are new creatures in Christ according to 2 Corinthians 5:17.

Putting off the old man involves putting good things and "God things" into your spirit man. Too many Christians fill up on spiritual junk food. Their diet consists of extreme end time teachings, political, cultural, or even carnal schools of thought. As a result they are deficient in their maturity. God is calling us to put *off* the old and put *in* the new!

Give your attention to the truths in this book and let yourself be encouraged to shed the skin of an old life and an old season. God has something better for you to step into…. But you've got to make room for it!

CHAPTER ONE
OLD SKIN

God's Design for Shedding

Snakes shed their skin. In fact the average snake sheds its skin about 4 times per year. The reason is quite simple: as the snake grows, it sheds old skin so that it can become bigger. It prevents the scales from tearing and ripping when the size of the snake increases. Likewise, if you're a sold-out believer in Jesus, you'll naturally want to grow and become *bigger* in God. We are called to be spiritual giants, not spiritual dwarfs. In order to grow, however, you've got to shed old skin to make room for growth.

See, when we get saved we instantly are converted and we become saints of God. However, that sainthood has to be walked out. As it's walked out, God deals with lots and lots of stuff in our lives. Old thinking, habits, vices, and ways of living are pushed out. He puts His finger on areas that need to change and in that moment we have the opportunity to either yield to His grace, shed the old skin, and make room for growth… or we stay as is with a hardened heart and experience the painful consequences of that decision.

We have to remember that salvation isn't a stopping place but a starting place. The process of renewing and putting off old ways isn't a one-time event at salvation but a continual one that never ends throughout the life of a Christian. Let me paint a picture: I would wager that as you read this, you probably took a shower or bath recently. I would hope so anyways.

You didn't necessarily have to go out and play in the mud or work a dirty job in order to need a bath. Simply living in the world and walking out your day to day life causes us to sweat and to need a shower at the end of the day. The principle is the exact same in the spirit.

We don't have to go out and backslide into deep dark sin to need the cleansing power of God. Just it's a matter of the offensive smell they were putting off!

Likewise, when Christians live in sin without repentance, they begin to smell spiritually. They aren't less than any other believer and they certainly don't lack value, however — their lifestyle puts off an offensive fragrance that isn't fun to be around. When a believers depart from righteous living and stray into sin, they sometimes gets offended and hurt that there is a parting-of-ways between them and the church. However, it isn't God's fault. It also isn't the church's fault.

As a matter of fact, it's the fault of the one who is choosing a *lifestyle contrary* to the life of the believer. They've got to put off the old man and his ways. As they do they'll find an awesome fellowship with God and with that comes an awesome fellowship with God's *people*.

"This I say, therefore, and testify in the Lord, that you should no longer walk as the rest of the Gentiles walk, in the futility of their mind…" (Ephesians 4:17)

There must be a change of walk when we come to Christ. The things that didn't previously phase us living in the world and going about our daily business causes us to need to be washed by the Lord continually.

AN EPHESIANS EXPOSITION

"…just as Christ also loved the church and gave Himself for her, that He might sanctify and cleanse her with the washing of water by the word." (Ephesians 5:25-26)

When you live in this world, the world gets on you. The way to be clean from the world is to continually cleanse yourself with the Word. If you don't continually get in the shower of God, so to speak, you'll start to experience a seared heart wherein you lose sensitivity to conviction. This is a dangerous place to be! When I played football in high school and college, some guys would take pride in not washing their practice uniforms all summer. They smelled horrendous. You didn't want to stand near them. In jest they'd say things like, "Are you too good to stand near me?" It's not a matter of being better than them, suddenly bother us. The compromises that used to be normal are now uncomfortable. If a Christian doesn't have a life that looks different from the world, they're not living up to the standard of the Christian label that they have on them. To be a Christian literally and simply means "Christ-like one." Let this distinction be your way of life. Let's continue:

"...having their understanding darkened, being alienated from the life of God, because of the ignorance that is in them, because of the blindness of their heart." (Ephesians 4:18)

We've been enlightened by the Spirit of God within us. Psalms talks about the Word of God being a light to our path. We have an illumination that the world doesn't have. As a result, we are able to live in a way that the world can't live.

Don't be surprised when sinners act like sinners. It's all that they know. A sinner can't live righteously. However, we can! We have shed the darkened understanding and ignorance that we used to wear daily. Our blinded hearts have been opened *to see again*. Just as much as sinners can't live righteously, we the righteous, shouldn't be able to live as sinners.

"

Just as much as sinners can't live righteously, we the righteous, shouldn't be able to live as sinners.

Don't let yourself be pulled back into the ignorance of the world. Otherwise you'll start to live accordingly. When I was in college, my major was working with mentally and physically handicapped people. I would work in schools and institutions to provide care and education to these folks. I noticed something interesting during my time in that field. No matter how mentally impaired a person was, if they were able to speak — they could cuss. Even if their IQ was 30, if they could form words — you bet they were going to swear.

Even though at the time I was a sinner, I had a revelation: you don't have to be very intelligent to cuss. However, it takes intelligence and integrity to be able to communicate clearly without profanity. That is what we are called to! Not the ignorance of the old man. Our spiritual IQ has increased, so to speak. We have the knowledge of God enabling us to live differently than before.

"…who, being past feeling, have given themselves over to lewdness, to work all uncleanness with greediness." (Ephesians 4:19)

Notice the phrase "being past feeling." It describes such a callousness that conviction of any kind isn't effective in bringing about change. How does a person get to this place? By failing to regularly maintain cleanliness through the Word. Hardening yourself to subtle conviction and leading will eventually leave you "past feeling" as Paul describes.

"But you have not so learned Christ, if indeed you have heard Him and have been taught by Him, as the truth is in Jesus." (Ephesians 4:20-21)

Over the years there have been many people who have taken positions as pastors and leaders and claimed to be "the Christ." Of course, they were false prophets who led people astray. Yet their followers were fully committed to them — believing whole heartedly that the person was indeed Jesus Christ. What happened? They learned *another* Christ. They didn't learn Christ through the Word and the Spirit. They learned a false Christ through deception.

It doesn't have to be as extreme as following a false leader claiming to be God. It can be as simple as learning an idea about the gospel that Jesus didn't teach.

For example, believing that you don't really have to stay committed to prayer and the Bible in order to live the Christian life falls into the "another Christ" category. Maybe you've subconsciously begun to think that those things are old fashioned and unnecessary. Maybe you've learned a concept that teaches in order to *win* the world you have to *emulate* the world. These things you didn't learn in Christ. You see, we have learned the true and living Christ by authentic means. As a result, we've gained an understanding of truth that has caused us to look completely different than the world.

"...that you *put off*, concerning your former conduct, the old man which grows corrupt according to the deceitful lusts, and be renewed in the spirit of your mind." (Ephesians 4:22-23 emphasis added)

Many years ago, the church saw these passages with more sincerity. Marriage for example, was taken much more seriously. "Til death do us part" was a literal, whole hearted declaration… not a flimsy greeting card. Decades ago it was understood that separation between the world and the church must take place. This doesn't mean segregation… just separation. What's the difference? Segregation means that we don't have contact with the world… which isn't the will of God. We should have lots of contact with the world. Separation merely means we won't *participate* in their behavior and lifestyle.

If you stay in the mix of the world for too long, the world will start to clothe you with sin and bad habits. Separation allows us to take time to be renewed and cleansed while still remaining influential in the world yet clean in God.

I got saved in my early twenties out of a hellacious lifestyle. I was a mess. When I committed myself to the Lord, I knew that if Christianity was anything like the sports I was familiar with — it would take total commitment, time and practice. This outlook on growing in God enabled me to be cleaned up and propelled forward in Christ, in my marriage, family, and ministry. I could have gotten saved, gotten my life cleaned up a bit, and then simply stayed there in a stagnant place. However, that isn't God's best.

Too many people come to Christ in a place of real pain. Once Jesus lifts just enough pain to make life livable again, they stop seeking after God and remain in a lukewarm Christian state. What a tragedy considering God has done everything He can do to cause us to live above this thinking and live in a continual state of renewal.

CHAPTER TWO

THE CATCH-UP

Catapulting the Mind to New Places

There are no if's, and's, or maybe's about it: Jesus is the passageway to salvation. When we get saved, it isn't our minds that get saved. It's our *spirit* that gets saved. As a result, our mind has to catch up. Our mind has to be renewed to the reality of our salvation. Why is this important? Because the passage in Ephesians 4 that we've been unpacking goes on to say:

"…and that you put on the new man which was created according to God, in true righteousness and holiness." (Ephesians 4:24)

How do we put off the old man? Or better yet, where do we put off the old man? In our minds. It's in our thinking that this takes place. The old man has been crucified and buried with Christ at our salvation according the Word. Yet we have to continually put him off in our thought process.

Our new man should be put on as a perpetual practice. The new man according to the verse prior was created according to God! Our new behavior, way of thinking and way of seeing has been patterned after Jesus Himself. That is not a bad upgrade!

Not only that, but we were created in *true* righteousness. I love that Paul included the word true to preface the word righteousness. Why? Because many people attempt to live out a falsified version of righteousness. It's their own attempt at godliness. For example some would say that it's righteous to not learn how to swim. Why? Because swimming would require a bathing suit which is ungodly in their eyes. Others might say not wearing makeup is righteous. Others might add that forbidding jewelry is holy. None of these things hold any water in the true Christian faith. They aren't founded in the true righteous pattern that Jesus ordained for our lives.

True righteousness works from the inside out. When you're in a relationship with Jesus, you'll know what's right and wrong for you. The Holy Ghost is quite capable of convicting you. The Bible says, "but now much more in my absence, work out your own salvation with fear and trembling" (Philippians 2:12 emphasis added).

Notice, we are to work out *our own* salvation. Meaning we have to sift through our standards and convictions. There is nothing wrong with preaching universal standards… in fact, we should! Yet they must be based on biblical principles, not personal quirks and preferences.

All of these things require a mental catch-up on our part. I've said for years that Christianity is a thinkers game. To do this thing right means that we have got to intentionally position our minds to think on the things that our salvation has made available. The salvation of our spirits is a free gift from God. The salvation of our minds is something that takes effort on our part, yet it isn't a works mentality. It's grace that makes this renewal available as we act on what we believe!

CHAPTER THREE
OUR ROLE

The User's Maintenance Manual

Our *change* is dependent upon our *learning*. This is apparent when Paul said, "…You have not so learned Christ…" In other words, your behavior is directly linked to what you've learned. This means we have responsibility in our sanctification. We don't have all of the responsibility, thank God. Certainly it is God who makes it happen and initiates it. However, we do carry a load in working out what God has made available.

How do I come to this conclusion? Because of the language Paul continually uses when instructing the church. "Put off the old man" and "put on the new man" are instructions directed at the individual believer. It isn't for God to put it on and off. It's for the believer to do so! God will not do for you what He has commissioned you to do for yourself. We need to do all that we can do and then God will do what only He can do.

> *God will not do for you what He has commissioned you to do for yourself.*

When Debbie and I were first married over 40 years ago, I didn't smoke but she did. If you know my wife, she is the sweetest thing and it's hard to even imagine a cigarette in her hand. Nevertheless, she did. I wouldn't even kiss her until she brushed her teeth. I would give her a hard time about it. Finally she decided to quit. For a year she would still have cravings. I think at times she would sit next to folks who were smoking just to get a little second-hand smoke. For a whole year she battled it. Cravings tried to hold on. Eventually the cravings subsided and she now absolutely abhors the smell of cigarette smoke, praise God. Her desires shifted and did a complete 180 as she put off old desires and put on new ones. It wasn't easy, yet she did it through persistence.

You see, there are things we must do that God will not do for us. He will help us, give grace, and assistance — yet a firm stance is required on our part. If you'll be sincere with God and submit and continue submitting, stuff will drop off your life and you'll get the victory in Jesus' name! Don't quit! Don't back down. Don't be condemned. Keep pushing ahead!

SELF CLEANSING

"And their message will spread like cancer. Hymenaeus and Philetus are of this sort, who have strayed concerning the truth, saying that the resurrection is already past; and they overthrow the faith of some." (2 Timothy 2:17-18)

Notice, the Bible says they strayed from the truth. That means they were once in the truth. If you aren't careful to guard what you have in God, you could lose it. These men were teaching that the rapture, essentially, had already taken place. It was defeating the faith of those who were listening and leaving them hopeless. The teaching doesn't have to be so drastic. For example, I love being an American citizen. I love our heritage and our story. I love the freedoms that we stand for. However, I am a Christian before I am an American.

If we aren't careful we can start to put our nationality above our faith. We can allow the freedoms that our country affords us to interfere with our standards in God. We could use our freedom of speech for evil instead of good. We could use our liberty to covet careers and money above Jesus, birthing greed in our hearts. Don't allow yourself to stray from the truth. Remain in it through the God-kind of maintenance that we are talking about. Let's continue:

"Nevertheless the solid foundation of God stands, having this seal: 'The Lord knows those who are His,' and, 'Let everyone who names the name of Christ depart from iniquity.' But in a great house there are not only vessels of gold and silver, but also of wood and clay, some for honor and some for dishonor. Therefore *if anyone cleanses himself* from the latter, he will be a vessel for honor, sanctified and useful for the Master, prepared for every good work." (2 Timothy 2:19-21 emphasis added)

The scripture explicitly says, "if anyone cleanses himself." It isn't a matter of God sovereignly taking control of your will and cleansing you. It's a matter of self-responsibility and cleansing yourself to be used!

"Flee also youthful lusts; but pursue righteousness, faith, love, peace with those who call on the Lord out of a pure heart. But avoid foolish and ignorant disputes, knowing that they generate strife. And a servant of the Lord must not quarrel but be gentle to all, able to teach, patient, in humility correcting those who are in opposition, if God perhaps will grant them repentance, so that they may know the truth, and that they may come to their senses and escape the snare of the devil, having been taken captive by him to do his will." (2 Timothy 2:22-26)

Change is tough. Men don't even like to change their socks. I've got three boys and a daughter.

Raising the boys was interesting. If they found a shirt that they favored, they would wear that shirt 5 or 6 days a week. They didn't like change. Most people don't. We like to keep our patterns. We are creatures of habit. This isn't a bad thing if our habits are healthy. However, being a creature of habit doesn't work for you but works against you when your habits are set on the things of the flesh. What the verse above is describing is us changing and breaking old-man driven habits and replacing them with a new-man driven lifestyle!

"

We are creatures of habit. This isn't a bad thing if our habits are healthy

CHAPTER FOUR
STAYING VS. STRAYING

Gaining a New Modus Operandi

Philip was sent to Samaria and a powerful city-wide revival broke out. Heaven bent low and kissed the earth and they got caught in the smack. Miracles, signs, and wonders were breaking out everywhere. In the midst of this, an issue arose with a man name Simon who was a sorcerer.

"But there was a certain man called Simon, who previously practiced sorcery in the city and astonished the people of Samaria, claiming that he was someone great, to whom they all gave heed, from the least to the greatest, saying, 'This man is the great power of God.'" (Acts 8:9-10)

Simon was no joke. He was an expert in false miracles and sorcery. He was so convincing that not only the gullible, poor, and uneducated fell for it, but the upper echelon of society bought in. As noted in verse 10, the people themselves said that he had the great power of God.

"And they heeded him because he had astonished them with his sorceries for a long time." (Acts 8:11)

It's one thing to astonish people for a one night show. It's a whole different story when you astonish people for a long time. In order to drop jaws over an extended period of time, you've got to upgrade your methods and tactics. In the world of sorcery, in order to upgrade your tactics — you've got to find someone who operates at a higher level than you and pay for the secrets. Simon was invested in this business. He likely spent a lot of money on his trade. It was his livelihood and his fame. Yet look what happened to him:

"But when they believed Philip as he preached the things concerning the kingdom of God and the name of Jesus Christ, both men and women were baptized. Then Simon himself also believed; and when he was baptized he continued with Philip, and was amazed, seeing the miracles and signs which were done." (Acts 8:12-12)

Simon himself believed! See, Simon knew fake. He knew sorcery. He knew the false version of power. Yet when Philip came to town preaching the good news of Christ, an authentic power had come. Simon was converted, baptized, and experienced God.

Yet interestingly enough, Simon's story didn't stop there. His entire life was spent on paying people for power and secrets, and then exploiting the common man for money. When Simon saw that the Holy Spirit was falling upon those whom Peter and John prayed for, he wanted in. Yet instead of realizing that what we receive in the kingdom is free, he fell into old habits and attempted to pay for that which came from the Lord.

"Now when the apostles who were at Jerusalem heard that Samaria had received the word of God, they sent Peter and John to them, who, when they had come down, prayed for them that they might receive the Holy Spirit. For as yet He had fallen upon none of them. They had only been baptized in the name of the Lord Jesus. Then they laid hands on them, and they received the Holy Spirit.

And when Simon saw that through the laying on of the apostles' hands the Holy Spirit was given, he offered them money, saying, 'Give me this power also, that anyone on whom I lay hands may receive the Holy Spirit.'" (Acts 8: 14-19)

It might sound odd to us that he offered money to the apostles to get this gift, and it should. However, this was Simon's upbringing. This was what he knew. His life had been surrounded by supernatural experiences being exchanged for money. Do you see how crucial it is that our old modes of operation die at the cross? Look at Peter's response:

"But Peter said to him, "Your money perish with you, because you thought that the gift of God could be purchased with money! You have neither part nor portion in this matter, for your heart is not right in the sight of God." (Acts 8:20-21)

Was Simon saved? Absolutely. He had believed and was baptized by Philip. However, his heart wasn't right with God. In fact, Peter went on to say, "Repent therefore of this your wickedness, and pray God if perhaps the thought of your heart may be forgiven you. For I see that you are poisoned by bitterness and bound by iniquity" (Acts 8:22-23).

He was poisoned by bitterness and bound by an old means of thinking. Just because he experienced conversion didn't mean that his life was put together immediately. He needed to be corrected by Peter and taught the Word and way of God. After that, he requested prayer from the Apostles. He wanted change. Yet church history tells us that Simon became a minister in opposition to the church, teaching heresy.

We don't know exactly how true that is but it is a strong possibility based on early church writers. The fact is, we can't attempt to live our entire Christian life based on one moment of repentance... it has to be a continual one.

Trying to live off of yesterday's revelation for the rest of your life is a recipe for straying. Israel had to receive fresh manna daily, otherwise the old manna would rot! We must receive fresh bread from heaven every single day.

> *"We can't attempt to live our entire Christian life based on one moment of repentance... it has to be a continual one.*

I've seen people be born again yet poisoned with bitterness. They have walked with Jesus for decades yet a hurtful event takes place and they become bound by offense. God deals with the matter, puts his finger on the place of hurt and they have the chance to repent again. (I deal with this is great detail in my book *Forgiveness: An Act of Violence*)

Don't think that you can survive the Christian walk without continual maintenance. Nobody has and nobody will. God has designed it to work and operate in the context of relationship and *relationship* demands continual fellowship and growth... not occasional fellowship and intermittent growth spurts.

CHANGING YOUR MODE OF OPERATION

We were raised and taught growing up to live certain ways. Maybe anger was your mode of operation, like it was for me. Maybe lying got you through your troubles. Perhaps threatening to kill yourself was a means of manipulation and gaining sympathy. There are so many false ideas about how to live life that we are taught by the world growing up. Yet despite all of this, it's absolutely paramount that we don't revert to old modes of operation after we get saved. Don't stray. Don't veer. Stay fixed on daily maintenance in Jesus' presence.

Let God structure new modes of operation in your heart. You won't default to sin and the old man, you'll instead default to the ways of the new man. You'll shed the old skin to make room for growth in God. This is your call! Live large in God and let God live large in you.

CHAPTER FIVE

MANDATORY MATURITY

A Look at Growing Up in God

Christianity has often been identified with the butterfly. This is because the Christian life is a process of transformation. It's a shifting from one thing to another. Like a caterpillar cocooning to eventually become a butterfly, so it is with us. In God, we take on such a change that we can be difficult to recognize by people who knew how we used to be. The change is so beautiful!

I've never seen anyone look at a caterpillar and say, "Wow look at how beautiful this is!" Little kids don't chase caterpillars. They step on them. However, kids chase the beauty of a butterfly. The final result of the butterfly taking flight is a beautiful thing.

So it is with us. In the world, folks didn't look at us and say, "Wow what a powerful example of integrity, humility and love." No, in fact it might have been just the opposite in many cases. Yet now that we've been transformed in Christ — our lives display something worth looking at and something worth chasing.

SPIRITUAL RUNGS

It doesn't matter how mature and responsible you are in life... when you get saved, you become an infant in the Lord and must grow up. We all start at the same place of infancy in Jesus and there are rungs on the ladder to climb up, so to speak.

When someone is a baby Christian, folks don't mind if they do something dumb or if they aren't acting properly. Everyone is willing to clean up the mess because they don't know any better. In many ways they aren't applying the truth because they haven't been *informed* of the truth. As they continue to develop, however, they enter a toddler phase of Christianity. They've gained more knowledge and can begin to apply what they know. They're starting to get their footing. They still make messes and people are willing to help them clean up their mess — but there are fewer people who are willing to do so.

After a while we start saying to them, "God gave you two legs. Walk on them. I can't carry you all the time." In this phase of the Christian life, much like dealing with a toddler, you have to sternly deal with folks. With Toddlers you have to grab their arms, pull them up, and practice walking with them. When they don't want to eat, you have to be stern and make them eat. Likewise, in mentoring spiritual toddlers — we have to be exhaustingly consistent in pulling them up and walking with them.

Unfortunately, many Christians never leave this stage of Christianity. If we saw a teenager walking around with a diaper on and a pacifier in their mouth, we would recognize that there is something wrong with that kid. Yet if we could see in the spirit, in many churches today, we would see people who have been saved for 20 years yet still carrying about with a diaper on and pacifier in their mouth. These things shouldn't be. We can't allow our process of growth to be stunted. It must be continued!

As a believer moves out of the toddler stage and begins to climb higher in God they reach the teenage stage of the Christian life. You could call it adolescence. In this place they know just enough to be dangerous to themselves and somebody else. What do I mean by that? They are familiar with all the rules and the ins and the outs, yet not necessarily gripped by a fully grown integrity to walk it out. Teens have a way of thinking that they can experiment with disobedience and not pay a price. In spiritual adolescence, many find themselves experimenting with worldly things as the flair and excitement of faith seems to wear off for them. This isn't every spiritual teen… just some.

Teens often feel self-sufficient and able to live life without mom and dad. While that might be true, life without mom and dad would prove to be costly and harmful to themselves. Spiritual teens have the temptation, often, to feel self-sufficient. Meaning they feel stable enough to figure life out on their own, when in reality it was realizing that we couldn't do it on our own that got us to salvation to begin with!

As you *go* through and *grow* through these phases and stages you start to enter young adulthood and eventually become a fully mature, stable Christian. In this place you are a powerhouse for God. Why? Because you're independent of others yet fully dependent on Jesus. You have to learn to be dependent on Jesus yet independent of others. What does this mean? Instead of waiting for other people to clean up your mess, you're able to go help others clean up theirs. This really is the goal of Christianity. It's for you to do for others what was done for you.

"

In this place you are a powerhouse for God. Why? Because you're independent of others yet fully dependent on Jesus.

This doesn't mean that you don't have help from other people or that you are somehow above getting assistance from a brother or sister in the Lord. It just means that even if you don't have someone around to keep you accountable, you still aren't going to ricochet and stray from Jesus.

One of the more frustrating points of discipleship is the realization that folks don't become stable in Christ simply because they got born-again. Folks don't mature in the spirit automatically… just like a baby doesn't become a mature adult automatically. For the first two years of a baby's life, it is 100% dependent on others. Everything it eats, everything it does, everything it doesn't do is tightly monitored and help is given around the clock. Even if a person gets saved in their later years and is mature in age, they still require the help that's given to spiritual infants.

If a baby isn't fed correctly it will develop deficiencies physically and mentally. I would say that the crucial times of proper feeding and discipleship take place early on in the spiritual walk. If this doesn't happen, a person will be hurt. As a result they will hurt others. I personally want to grow in the Lord so that I can feed people properly. As a result they'll grow properly without deficiency... and from there they'll feed other infants with good spiritual food. The cycle and process continues until Jesus comes back!

CHAPTER SIX

DEVELOPING YOUR SOIL

Becoming Good Earth for God's Seed

"Then He spoke many things to them in parables, saying: "Behold, a sower went out to sow. And as he sowed, some seed fell by the wayside; and the birds came and devoured them. Some fell on stony places, where they did not have much earth; and they immediately sprang up because they had no depth of earth.

But when the sun was up they were scorched, and because they had no root they withered away. And some fell among thorns, and the thorns sprang up and choked them. But others fell on good ground and yielded a crop: some a hundredfold, some sixty, some thirty. He who has ears to hear, let him hear!" (Matthew 13:3-9)

This parable has been taught in a number of ways. You could emphasize the sower. You could bring out principles about the seed. You could talk about the Word. You might even teach on the yield.

However, I want to mention the soil. When we were born-again, we were shallow ground. Many get saved for shallow or selfish reasons. For example, you might have come to Jesus because you needed a disaster cleaned up. Maybe you got saved because you wanted a better life. The reality is, we are called to approach God for who He is, not just what we can get. Yet this shallow ground is there. So, our job is to cultivate it and deepen our soil, so to speak. We are called to prepare our hearts for the Word through prayer and anticipation. In this, God's Word will find deep soil in our hearts that He can plant into!

You can fertilize ground, you can put nutrients in it and so forth to cause it to produce more. Listen, if you're bad ground — you can change your ground! You'll no longer be shallow ground but excellent ground to carry the seed of God. Allow the Holy

Spirit to plow your heart. Get into the Scriptures and begin to let Jesus make up for what lacks in your heart. Remember the passage in 2 Timothy that we read? It said, "If anyone cleanses himself, he will be a vessel for honor." It's our job to do so. It's our responsibility to determine what kind of soil we will be.

Doubtless, in our society we have a victim mentality. We want to blame mom and dad, society, the church, God and anyone else. Yet God set up the system in such a way that we have to take responsibility for our actions. Our world is the result of the choices we've made. The soil of our hearts is determined by the steps we took to make it that way. Let yourself be good ground that's able to receive seed!

"

The soil of our hearts is determined by the steps we took to make it that way.

Even if other people in the Lord consider you to be mature, don't settle and stop there. Place a demand on yourself to climb higher. Realize that you haven't figured it all out yet. Understand that you haven't arrived and won't arrive on this side of heaven. Those who continue are in a constant learning process. As long as you are willing to submit to God and learn from God, He will provide revelation and insight to strengthen you and encourage you.

God gave you life. God gave you faith. What you do with your life is up to you. What you do with your faith is up to you. What you do with the faith God gave you is your gift back to God. What you do with what you have is your way of showing gratitude toward the things God has given you.

For Debbie and I, we started out in the basement spiritually. We needed a miracle just to be normal and at ground level. We needed a powerful move of God just to be stable and above water. Once we got to be normal, we continued to push for miracles and grow in the things of God. We didn't grow because we were ministers or because we were called to be pastors. No, we grew because we stayed planted in God.

> "Blessed is the man
> Who walks not in the counsel of the ungodly,
> Nor stands in the path of sinners,
> Nor sits in the seat of the scornful;
> But his delight is in the law of the Lord,
> And in His law he meditates day and night.
> He shall be like a tree
> *Planted by the rivers of water,*
> That brings forth its fruit in its season,
> Whose leaf also shall not wither;
> And whatever he does shall prosper." (Psalm 1:1-3 emphasis added)

The first rule of spiritual growth is to stay *planted*. If you take a plant and continue to uproot it and move it around from one soil plot to the next, it will die. It can only grow as it should when it remains planted in good ground. I watch people begin to grow in God yet as soon as God starts pressing in on their character flaws and issues — they uproot themselves from church and move somewhere else as if to escape God. As a result they wither spiritually instead of allowing God to treat the soil to cause better growth.

Notice, the tree in Psalm 1 is prosperous because it's planted by the river. A tree that isn't near the river won't benefit from the river. Just because God and the church are moving in the earth doesn't mean you'll reap the benefits of it. You'll have to intentionally make the choice to grow and plant yourself near the river of God in your life.

Living as a Christian requires focus. The word says, "...he is a double-minded man, unstable in all his ways" (James 1:8). A double-minded person who isn't focused on the single pursuit of God will be full of instability and shakiness. The devil will try everything he can to break your focus and throw distractions in your face.

On Sunday mornings, my job is to preach the Word. That requires focus. We are very interactive with our people at church. Before and after service we greet folks, talk, give hugs, and hang out with the people. We don't hide in the green room. However, I still have to work to maintain focus on Sunday mornings. I can't allow conversations and issues to distract from what the Lord has given me to do. Likewise, with any pursuit or venture in the Christian life, it requires focus and diligence to complete the task. Focus is a recipe for growth.

CHAPTER SEVEN
THE COST

Walking in Willingness to Sacrifice

After getting saved, friends and family often will see you as you were... not as you are. They often will do very little to help you mature and change. Sometimes they'll actually attempt to keep you as you were. Why? Because it doesn't put any pressure on them to change and climb higher. One of the biggest hurdles you'll climb as you grow is forgetting about what people think of you and focusing on what Jesus thinks of you.

Your new friends will seldom be your old friends. What does that mean? If you are going to go on with God, you can't stay in the seat of sinners. Should you be friends with sinners to influence them? Sure! Yet the vast majority of your time should not be with those in darkness, lest you start to wear that same darkness. Unwarranted time with old friends will produce old patterns in you. You have to keep a healthy balance when trying to win over folks from your old life.

"

Unwarranted time with old friends will produce old patterns in you.

A lot of people won't give up what they *were* to become what they *are*. It hurts to leave people you love. It is painful to depart from relationships that are harming you. It's tough to not have the conversations and jokes you used to with certain people. Yet it'll keep you, hold you, and maintain you in the clench of God! It's a worthwhile sacrifice. Some people say, "Yeah but Jesus made the sacrifice so I shouldn't have to!" No. You're called to be like him. We are called to share in his suffering and become familiar with sacrifice.

When you first start out in marriage and have no kids, you basically are able to do what you want to do when you want to do it. Yet as children are added to the picture, you have less rights and more responsibility. The sacrifice increases. As a pastor I have to ask myself, "Do I want to have a large church?" I know that as more people come in the door, we as a church give up more rights and take on more responsibility. Yet we cannot stay small while people are in darkness. We have to accept the responsibility for the lives that are brought to us and gladly make the sacrifices that maturity and growth require!

Sanctification is a super involved process that will take sweat and tears on your part. Yet it won't be a matter of your own strength or genius getting it done. It will be done in the flow of God's grace. Just like a track runner has fuel in his or her body to sprint quickly, you and I have fuel in our tank called grace. The job of growing up in God won't get done without grace, and it also won't get done without our effort. Jesus said, "where much is given, much is required." We have been given much in our salvation. Now it's time to fill the requirements of the "much" that we've been given. Put off the old man, stay steadfast in the truth and commit to the continual maintenance required in this beautiful thing called the Christian life.

MEET THE AUTHOR

Pastor John B. Lowe II has been faithful in the full time ministry for over 35 years. He carries a heart for the local church in Warsaw, yet has reached a world wide audience, ministering in many nations of the world, leading pastors conferences, marriage conferences, faith meetings, and more. Pastor and his lovely wife, Debbie, have four children and three daughter-in-laws who all serve God. They have several grandchildren and reside in Warsaw as pastors of New Life Christian Church & World Outreach

ALSO FROM
PASTOR JOHN B. LOWE:

FORGIVENESS: AN ACT OF VIOLENCE

*AVAILABLE ON AMAZON

NOTES

Newness: A Guide to Renewing the Mind and Putting Off the Old Man... for Good

Copyright © 2018 John B. Lowe II

Pulpit to Page Publishing Co.
USA & Abroad || PULPITTOPAGE.COM

Made in the USA
Columbia, SC
06 December 2018